SUPERMAN
NEW KRYPTON

SUPERMAN
NEW KRYPTON

VOLUME **ONE**

//FROM A CUB TO A WOLF

JAMES ROBINSON<WRITER>
JESUS MERINO//LENO CARVALHO//STEVE SCOTT
<PENCILLERS>
JESUS MERINO//NELSON PEREIRA//KEVIN STOKES
<INKERS>
LEE LOUGHRIDGE<COLORIST>
SAL CIPRIANO<LETTERER>

//THE WORST NIGHT OF HIS LIFE

JAMES ROBINSON<WRITER>
PERE PÉREZ<ARTIST>
DAVID BARON<COLORIST>
JOHN J. HILL<LETTERER>

//NEW KRYPTON

GEOFF JOHNS//JAMES ROBINSON//STERLING GATES
<WRITERS>
PETE WOODS//GARY FRANK//RENATO GUEDES
<PENCILLERS>
PETE WOODS//JON SIBAL//JOSÉ WILSON MAGALHÃES
<INKERS>
HI-FI<COLORIST>
STEVE WANDS<LETTERER>

//STRANGE MEETINGS
AND CHANCE ENCOUNTERS

JAMES ROBINSON<WRITER>
RENATO GUEDES<PENCILLER>
JOSÉ WILSON MAGALHÃES<INKER>
DAVID CURIEL<COLORIST>
JOHN J. HILL<LETTERER>

//BEYOND DOOMSDAY

GEOFF JOHNS<WRITER>
PETE WOODS<ARTIST>
BRAD ANDERSON<COLORIST>
ROB LEIGH<LETTERER>

<SUPERMAN>CREATED BY JERRY SIEGEL AND JOE SHUSTER

//
DAN DIDIO ‹SENIOR VP-EXECUTIVE EDITOR›
MATT IDELSON ‹EDITOR-ORIGINAL SERIES›
NACHIE CASTRO ‹ASSOCIATE EDITOR-ORIGINAL SERIES›
BOB HARRAS ‹EDITOR-COLLECTED EDITION›
ROBBIN BROSTERMAN ‹SENIOR ART DIRECTOR›
PAUL LEVITZ ‹PRESIDENT & PUBLISHER›
GEORG BREWER ‹VP-DESIGN & DC DIRECT CREATIVE›
RICHARD BRUNING ‹SENIOR VP-CREATIVE DIRECTOR›
PATRICK CALDON ‹EXECUTIVE VP-FINANCE & OPERATIONS›
CHRIS CARAMALIS ‹VP-FINANCE›
JOHN CUNNINGHAM ‹VP-MARKETING›
TERRI CUNNINGHAM ‹VP-MANAGING EDITOR›
AMY GENKINS ‹SENIOR VP-BUSINESS & LEGAL AFFAIRS›
ALISON GILL ‹VP-MANUFACTURING›
DAVID HYDE ‹VP-PUBLICITY›
HANK KANALZ ‹VP-GENERAL MANAGER, WILDSTORM›
JIM LEE ‹EDITORIAL DIRECTOR-WILDSTORM›
GREGORY NOVECK ‹SENIOR VP-CREATIVE AFFAIRS›
SUE POHJA ‹VP-BOOK TRADE SALES›
STEVE ROTTERDAM ‹SENIOR VP-SALES & MARKETING›
CHERYL RUBIN ‹SENIOR VP-BRAND MANAGEMENT›
ALYSSE SOLL ‹VP-ADVERTISING & CUSTOM PUBLISHING›
JEFF TROJAN ‹VP-BUSINESS DEVELOPMENT, DC DIRECT›
BOB WAYNE ‹VP-SALES›
//

Cover by GARY FRANK and JON SIBAL colored by BRAD ANDERSON
Publication design by ROBBIE BIEDERMAN

SUPERMAN: NEW KRYPTON volume 1
Published by DC Comics. Cover and compilation Copyright © 2009
DC Comics. All Rights Reserved.

Originally published in single magazine form in SUPERMAN'S PAL,
JIMMY OLSEN SPECIAL 1, ADVENTURE COMICS SPECIAL FEATURING THE
GUARDIAN 1, SUPERMAN: NEW KRYPTON SPECIAL 1, SUPERMAN 681, ACTION
COMICS 871 Copyright © 2008, 2009 DC Comics. All Rights Reserved.
All characters, their distinctive likenesses and related elements
featured in this publication are trademarks of DC Comics. The
stories, characters and incidents featured in this publication
are entirely fictional. DC Comics does not read or accept
unsolicited submissions of ideas, stories or artwork.

DC Comics, 1700 Broadway, New York, NY 10019
A Warner Bros. Entertainment Company
Printed in the USA. First Printing.
HC ISBN: 978-1-4012-2329-8
SC ISBN: 978-1-4012-2330-4

<FROM A CUB TO A WOLF> COVER ART BY RYAN SOOK

FOUR DAYS AGO.

NOT *EVERY* BAR PLAYS CONSTANT POGUES, DANNY, SORRY TO TELL YOU.

FINE, I'LL GIVE YOU THAT, BUT YOU--

--YOU'VE CHANGED, MAN.

CHANGED... *HOWSO?*

WELL, YOU WERE *FUN* ONCE UPON A TIME. NOW...

NO, KYLE, *I'LL* SAY IT. 'BOUT TIME *HE* HEARD IT TOO. JIMMY--

I'M *SURE* I'M NOT, DANNY. DAN. CALM DOWN.

YEAH MAN, *CHILL* OUT.

I'M *SORRY* FOR THE WAY I'M BEING GUYS, IT'S JUST THAT I'VE GOT STUFF IN MY HEAD.

WHAT? *GIRL* TROUBLE?

NO. I HAVE A GIRL. SORT OF. I MEAN I'M *SEEING* SOMEONE AND SHE'S A GIRL, SO--

NO, I HAVE A STORY... FOR THE DAILY PLANET, *MAYBE.* SOMEONE WILL LISTEN.

JIMMY IT'S *YOUR* TURN.

I'LL PASS, GUYS.

BUT IT WAS *YOUR* IDEA TO COME TO AN ENGLISH PUB IN THE FIRST PLACE. I'M IRISH, FOR HEAVEN'S SAKE. AND THEY'RE PLAYING THE *BUZZCOCKS*, WHO I HATE EVEN THOUGH THE HIPSTER POWERS-THAT-BE HAVE *DECLARED* THEM ALL-TIME GREATS.

KENT. KANT WAS A PHILOSOPHER AND I *NEVER* MENTION HIM.

SEE? *THAT.* YOU THINK YOU'RE *BETTER... SMARTER* THAN ME.

--WHEN YOU'RE *NOT* TALKING ABOUT SUPERMAN YOU'RE TALKING ABOUT THAT KANT GUY.

I'M JOKING.

YEAH, WELL YOU'RE *NOT* SMARTER THAN ME.

I AGREE, DANNY. NEXT TO YOU I'M A MENTAL *LILLIPUTIAN.*

IF I *COMPLETELY* UNDERSTOOD WHAT YOU JUST SAID, I'D *MAYBE* SHOW YOU YOU'RE NOT AS GOOD A FIGHTER AS ME, TOO.

YOU'RE GROWING *APART* FROM ME AND THE GUYS, JIM.

MAYBE.

MAYBE I'M JUST GROWING UP.

MAYBE IT'S JUST THAT I'M GROWING UP, JIMMY.

BUT I CAN'T HANG AROUND ANYMORE WAITING FOR YOU TO STEP UP.

AS IN WHAT? MARRIAGE? WE'VE BEEN TOGETHER FOR LIKE NO TIME AT ALL AND WE'RE YOUNG...WAY TOO YOUNG FOR WALKING DOWN THE AISLE.

I DIDN'T MEAN THAT.

I MEANT...JUST...YOU SEE ME, WE HOOK UP, YOU GO OR I DO.

I KNOW YOU DON'T LOVE ME, BUT DO YOU EVEN LIKE ME?

SURE I DO. YOU'RE COOL.

IT'S JUST I HAVE STUFF IN MY HEAD.

LET ME GUESS. SUPERMAN... "YOUR BEST BUDD" CLARK KENT "YOU NEXT BEST BUDD" THEN "MISS" LOI LANE," THEN "PER WHITE," THEN, THEN, THEN.

OH.

THAT IT? NOT "NO"? NOT "BABY, NO"?

I GUESS NOT.

GOOD LUCK WITH YOUR CRAZY WORLD, JIMMY.

I'LL THINK OF YOU WHILE I'M LIVING IN MY SAFE ONE.

THIS IS BIGGER. I'M ON TO SOMETHING.

ME TOO. I'M ON TO A NEW JOB IN MIDWAY CITY. SALON... REALLY COOL UP-AND-COMING SALON THERE, NEEDS A COLORIST. THEY OFFERED ME THE JOB AND I'M GOING.

OLSEN!

OLSEN...THIS COFFEE'S **COLDER** THAN A WIDOW'S SHEETS.

IT WAS **HOT** WHEN I HANDED IT TO HIM. **WHY** DOESN'T HE DRINK IT WHEN HE **FIRST** GETS IT?

I'LL GET YOU A **REFILL**, CHIEF. SORRY.

RED-EYE, IF YOU'RE GOING JIMBO.

YES, MR. LOMBARD.

THIS STORY. I **HAVE** SOMETHING. I'M **SURE** I DO, BUT-- **WHO'D** LISTEN? PERRY ALREADY THINKS I'M AN IDIOT.

CLARK, SORRY, BUDDY, I **ALMOST** FORGOT--CAN I GET YOU SOMETHING TOO?

NO THANKS, I'M PICKY WITH MILK AND TEMPERATURE AND STUFF.

I JUST **WISH** I COULD TALK TO SOMEONE ABOUT THIS.

TELL YOU WHAT, I'LL COME ALONG.

BACK IN FIVE, PERRY.

WHAT IS IT, JIMMY?

WHAT DO YOU *MEAN,* CLARK?

I CAN *SEE* ON YOUR FACE THAT YOU NEED TO TALK.

I'M A GOOD *LISTENER.*

I *THINK* I HAVE A STORY. A REAL *HOT* ONE, TOO, BUT I DON'T KNOW FOR SURE AND I'M *SCARED* TO TELL PERRY 'CAUSE HE THINKS I'M NUTS AND MAYBE I AM.

SO TELL *ME* INSTEAD.

DO YOU *REMEMBER* THE FIGHT BETWEEN SUPES AND ATLAS?

HOW COULD I FORGET?

REMEMBER HOW SUPERGIRL CAME TO *HELP* AND SHE *IMMEDIATELY* GOT SICK AND HAD TO FLY AWAY?

SURE I DO...IT WAS ON TV.

WELL, ABOUT THAT TIME, I *SAW* A FIGURE UP ON THE ROOFTOPS.

HE'D COME AND GO, HERE AND THERE. BUT I GOT THE *DISTINCT* IMPRESSION HE WAS INVOLVED WITH SUPERGIRL'S *SUDDEN* WEAKNESS.

I WAS SHOOTING PICTURES *ALL* AROUND--TRYING TO GET A *DECENT* SNAP OF HIM, AND WITH THE PUSHING AND SHOVING FROM THE CROWD AND ME TRYING TO SNAP PIX OF SUPES AND ATLAS AT THE SAME TIME (OR PERRY WOULD HAVE *KILLED* ME), I COULDN'T REALLY TELL *WHAT* I WAS GETTING UNTIL LATER.

BUT I'M *GUESSING* YOU GOT SOMETHING.

EMPTY ROOFTOPS *MAINLY*, BUT I DID GET *TWO* SHOTS OF SOMETHING MORE.

I *ZOOMED* IN FOR A FEW-- WHICH IS A *GAMBLE* IF THE SUBJECT'S MOVING, BUT ANYWAY--I GOT THE GUY'S FACE.

SO *WHO* IS HE?

I'LL *GET* TO THAT. LET ME SHOW YOU THE *SECOND* PICTURE FIRST. HERE HE IS AS A *FULL* FIGURE--USED A *WIDER* LENS HERE--ANYWAY, LOOK, LIKE I SAID HE'S *UP* AMONG THE ROOFTOPS--

--BUT HE *ISN'T* STANDING ON ONE.

SO I'D DONE WHAT I WAS **SUPPOSED** TO DO...WHAT CLARK SAID...

AND I'D STOOD UP TO PERRY IN THE PROCESS, ALTHOUGH I COULD TELL EVEN **THEN** THAT NO WAY WAS I GOING TO MAKE A HABIT OF IT.

BUT FROM THERE...**WHAT?** I HAD THE NAME **JONATHAN DREW**, BUT AS I'D TOLD CLARK, HIS TRAIL HAD DRIED UP SOON AFTER HIS SISTER'S FUNERAL.

THEN INSPIRATION HIT ME.

I LOOKED AT THE PHOTO OF DREW AT THE FUNERAL **AGAIN**, SAW HOW IT'D BEEN CROPPED WHEN THE PLANET PRINTED IT FOR THE NEWSPAPER STORY, KEEPING DREW IN FRAME, BUT HALF-CROPPING ANOTHER MAN.

MORE HUNTING AROUND MY PLACE FOLLOWED--LOOKING THROUGH **ALL** MY NEGS OF OLD WORK, AND OF COURSE THE ONE I NEEDED WAS IN THE LAST BOX **AGAIN**.

BUT UPON BLOWING IT UP, I **GOT** WHAT I NEEDED--THE FULL PICTURE, SO TO SPEAK.

AND WITH THAT NEW FACE, I SOON UNCOVERED A **NEW** NAME...

IT HAS EVERYTHING.

JONATHAN DREW.

CODENAME: ASSASSIN.

COLONEL JONATHAN DREW, ASSASSIN.

COLONEL? AS IN *MILITARY*.

NOT LONG AFTER HIS *FIRST* EXPLOIT AS A SUPERHERO, MEN APPROACHED HIM--FILLED HIS HEAD WITH *IDEALS*. EVEN AT THE START JON WAS A *LOST* SOUL--ESPECIALLY AFTER HIS SISTER DIED--LIKE I SAID, *READ* THE FILE.

LIKE I SAID, I'M *DONE*--

KRAK

I SEE STONE DIE, THEN I *DIVE* FOR MY LIFE.

I'M NOT SURE WHAT TO EXPECT *NEXT*--

WHERE ARE YOU, OLSEN?

AND *WHY* CAN'T I READ YOUR MIND?

I TAKE LIKE, A MOMENT--NO, I'M LYING WHEN I SAY A MOMENT--LIKE FOUR HOURS OF LYING ON THE FLOOR OF MY APARTMENT CLUTCHING MY CHEST--

--AND THEN I LOOK AT STONE'S FILE.

IT BEGINS WITH A TALE. IT'S THE ORIGIN OF A HERO--KIND OF A HERO, I MEAN--WHO GIVES HIMSELF A HERO NAME OF CODENAME: ASSASSIN?

BUT FROM THE BEGINNING IT'S OBVIOUS JONATHAN DREW WAS FAR FROM NORMAL. HOW HE BECAME WHAT HE BECAME IS THE SAME SET OF CHANCE CIRCUMSTANCES AND CRAZINESS THAT LED TO THE CREATION OF MANY A MEMBER OF THE JLA, SO WHO AM I TO JUDGE--

--BUT STILL, THIS TALE IS WHACKED OUT EVEN BY SUPERHERO CRAZY STANDARDS.

JONATHAN DREW, STUDENT, ORPHAN, ONLY PERSON IN THE WORLD HE HAS IS HIS SISTER.

SHE LOVES HIM BACK. SHE'S A LAWYER. SHE THINKS SHE'S REPRESENTING ITALIAN BUSINESSMEN. NO. GUESS WHAT, SHE'S IN BED WITH THE MOB. AND SHE DOESN'T KNOW. OR MAYBE SHE DOES.

THAT'S THE QUESTION THAT CAN'T BE ANSWERED BECAUSE THE MOB, THINKING SHE KNOWS TOO MUCH, HAS HER KILLED.

MEANWHILE--NO--JUST **BEFORE** THIS-- JONATHAN AGREES TO SOME TESTS ON HIS BRAIN, PSYCHIATRIC STUFF **MIXED** WITH MAD SCIENCE--NO WONDER STONE WAS SENT INTO THE **CORNFIELD**--ANYWAY HE'S STRAPPED INTO SOME KIND OF BRAIN SENSOR, **GIZMO** CONTRAPTION--

--THAT TRUE, TO SUPERHERO CHANCE ORIGINS, **PROMPTLY** BLOWS UP.

DREW SURVIVES.

AND **NOW** HE'S THE PIMP DADDY OF TELEKINESIS. HE CAN **BLOW** YOUR MIND WITH A THOUGHT, HE CAN **WALK** ON AIR, HE CAN DO A LOT OF STUFF.

AND WHAT HE DOES **FIRST** IS GET A FANCY COSTUME AND A WEIRD CHOICE OF NAME FOR A SECRET IDENTITY AND GO **OUT** AND GET REVENGE FOR HIS SISTER.

FIGHTS A COUPLE OF SECOND-RATE VILLAINS. **POWERHOUSE** AND **THE SNAKE.** KILLS THEM.

HE RETURNS TO STONE. HE'S **INTENT** ON CONTINUING THIS SUPERHERO, HARDCORE, **REVENGE** AGAINST BAD-GUYS THING--

--AND **THEN** GENTLEMEN WITH BROAD SHOULDERS IN DRAB SUITS WITH HIGH CLEARANCE (**MILITARY-WISE**) COME CALLING.

THEY **SMILE** AND MAKE HIM THEIR FRIEND AND FILL HIS HEAD WITH **IDEAS.**

DREW GOES **AWAY** WITH THE BROAD-SHOULDERED MEN.

STONE GETS ONE CARD FROM DREW LATER SAYING HE'S HAPPY AND HE'S ARMY AND HE'S *JUST* MADE COLONEL.

AND THAT'S *THAT,* EXCEPT ONE THING--NO *TWO* THINGS, I GUESS--

DREW--*WHEN* HE WAS CODENAME: ASSASSIN, WITH ALL HIS MENTAL POWERS, *STILL* HAD SOME VERY *STATE-OF-THE-ART* WEAPONRY HE WAS *MORE* THAN HAPPY TO USE.

STONE *ALWAYS* WONDERED *WHERE* A COLLEGE STUDENT FOUND THAT STUFF AND WONDERED HOW *EARLY* THE ARMY WERE INTO HIM.

AND THEN, ON *ONE* DAY WHEN THE BROAD-SHOULDERED SUITS WERE DOING THEIR *THING*--

TWO OF THEM WENT OFF, *SPOKE* OUT OF STONE'S EARSHOT.

WHAT THEY *DIDN'T* KNOW WAS THAT STONE HAD WORKED IN A CLINIC FOR THE DEAF AT AN EARLIER POINT IN HIS LIFE.

AT THAT TIME, HE'D *TRIED* TO LEARN HOW TO LIP-READ.

SURE HE WAS NO *WHIZ* AT IT, BUT HE'D LEARNED ENOUGH THAT AS THE BROAD-SHOULDERED MEN WHISPERED HE CAUGHT A WORD OR TWO.

CADMUS. *WALTER JOHNSON.* AND ONE OF THE MEN SPEAKING WAS NAMED *WINTERBOURNE.*

FACTS IN A FILE FOR STONE.

TO ME THEY WERE *NAMES*-- NAMES I *KNEW.*

THE FIRST--WALTER JOHNSON. HIS SON, **FLIP**, HAD BEEN AN **ADDITION** TO THE **NEW** WAVE OF THE NEWSBOY LEGION. FLIP WAS WALTER'S **SON**, AS I FIRST WAS TOLD AND THOUGHT AND BELIEVED, AS WERE ALL THE NEW "NEWSBOYS"--SONS OF THEIR FATHERS.

LIKE **STEPPING STONES** ACROSS A STREAM-- ONE-- TWO--THREE--

I WAS BEGINNING TO PUT **PIECES** TOGETHER. LIKE A **REAL** REPORTER-- **ALL** THE WHILE AWARE THAT ANY MOMENT I COULD GET MY FEET **WET**.

AND THEN I LEARNED THEY WERE **CLONES**. COPIES. CADMUS' STOCK IN TRADE. AH, THE **CADMUS** PROJECT.

STILL--I TAKE MY **FIRST** HOP/SKIP-- FROM STONE TO THE NAMES HE LISTS THAT I **KNOW**.

BUT I WAS THEIR **FRIEND**--THE "KIDS"--FOR A TIME. **CRAZY** TIME. FUN TIME. THAT **EVEN** AT MY YOUNG AGE NOW SEEMS LIKE A **FAIRY TALE** FROM LONG AGO.

STILL, I DID--DO KNOW WALTER JOHNSON, SCIENTIST. **RETIRED**, SURE, BUT HE WAS STILL A CONTACT.

"WAS" BEING THE **RIGHT** WORD--

WALTER HAD BEEN *MURDERED*. BY *DREW*, I'M GUESSING.

I FEAR THE *WORST* FOR THE *OTHER* ORIGINAL NEWSBOY LEGIONNAIRES.

AND I'M *RIGHT* TO BE AFRAID.

THEY'RE *DEAD*. MURDERED. *ALL* OF THEM.

DREW TAKES HIS *"CODENAME"* SERIOUSLY.

SO THAT LEFT CADMUS...

...A PLACE OF SCIENCE, A PLACE OF DISCOVERY, CRAZY AND WILD AND ALIVE.

THIS WAS NOT WHAT I RECALLED.

THERE'S NO ONE HERE. NOT A MAN TO BE FOUND.

NO, ONE SOUL REMAINS BEHIND.

--AND ALTHOUGH CALLING HIM A MAN MIGHT BE PUSHING IT, I CAN AT LEAST ATTEST TO HIS GOOD HEART.

DUBBILEX. CLONED ALIEN. ALIEN CLONE. I NEVER *COULD* WORK OUT *WHICH* HE WAS. AND EVEN WHEN CADMUS WAS ABUZZ HE SEEMED TO KEEP HIMSELF. *ALONE.*

NOW HE *REALLY* IS. HE SITS IN AN OFFICE AS BARE AS THE REST OF THE PLACE.

THE FLOOR AROUND HIS DESK IS SOAKED WITH *WATER.* MY FEET ARE WET, AFTER ALL.

I'M A *CUSTODIAN* OF NOTHING, JIMMY.

THE ARMY HAS TAKEN *EVERYTHING.* ALL OF CADMUS' CLONING DATA-- ALL THE EQUIPMENT--

HOW IS THAT POSSIBLE? CAN THE MILITARY JUST--

THEY CAME WITH A *BIG* COLLECTION OF ACQUISITION FORMS AND A *BIGGER* COLLECTION OF MEN. ALL ARMED.

THE *ONLY* THING THEY LEFT WAS ME.

ONE OF THE MEN MADE THE CRACK THAT THE *LAST* THING THEY NEEDED WAS AN ALIEN WHEN KILLING *ANOTHER* ALIEN WAS THEIR AGENDA.

HMM.

DOES THE NAME DREW MEAN ANYTHING TO YOU?

JONATHAN DREW? HE WAS OUR FIRST HEAD OF SECURITY--FOR LIKE A MINUTE AND FIFTEEN SECONDS--LONG BEFORE YOU CAME ON THE SCENE.

WELL HE'S GOOD AT KILLING, SO I'M SURE THINGS WERE SECURE.

OH, JIMMY, IF YOU ONLY KNEW.

SIGH

AND I GUESS IT'S TIME YOU DID.

"*BACK* WHEN CADMUS WAS *YOUNG*--WHEN THE NEWSBOYS WERE FIRST MEN--

"--THEY DISCOVERED BY TESTING ON THEM-SELVES--AND THEIR FRIEND *JIM HARPER*--THAT SOME PEOPLE ARE *SPECIAL*.

"HARPER WAS *ONE* SUCH PERSON.

"CADMUS ASKED HIM FOR *MORE* TESTS. HE AGREED--*EVER* THE PUBLIC SERVANT--EVER THE *GUARDIAN*.

"I DON'T KNOW *WHAT* HE THOUGHT THE TESTS HE WENT THROUGH MIGHT *HELP* PROVIDE.

"THE 'BOYS' HAD SIGNED OFFICIAL FORMS *FORBIDDING* THEM TO TELL THE TRUTH, AND THEY WERE *TRUE* TO THEIR OATHS FOR A TIME.

"BUT HARPER WAS THEIR FRIEND AND THEY WERE *TRUER* TO HIM IN THE END.

"THEY TOLD HIM.

"AND *SO* BEGAN THE *LAST* ADVENTURE OF THE ORIGINAL GUARDIAN."

HELLO. I *DIDN'T* THINK WE'D SEE EACH OTHER AGAIN.

CADMUS. THEN.

CADMUS--FIVE MINUTES *PRIOR* TO THEN.

FATE. KISMET. GOOD OLD-FASHIONED *BAD* LUCK. THE CHIEF EXECUTIVE OFFICER OF SECURITY THAT NIGHT WAS *AWAY* AT THE TIME HARPER BREACHED THE ENCLAVE OF CADMUS.

"BUT HE *ARRIVED* SOON AFTER THE FACT.

"AND HE *FOLLOWED* A TRAIL OF UNCONSCIOUS MEN.

"STEP BY STEP.

"MAN BY MAN.

"AND *FOUND* THE REASON FOR IT ALL.

SO THE TALE OF JIM HARPER BEING A COP KILLED IN THE LINE OF DUTY WAS A *LIE*.

NOT IF YOU CONSIDER HARPER HAVING A DUTY TO HIMSELF.

BUT *NEEDLESS* TO SAY, DREW *OVERSTEPPED* HIS AUTHORITY. IF ANYONE BUT HARPER HAD BREACHED THE INNER SANCTUM--THERE MIGHT HAVE BEEN *ANOTHER* ROW OF RIBBONS ON HIS CHEST. KILL THE GOLDEN GOOSE--DREW WAS *GONE* QUICKER THAN JAY GARRICK AFTER BAD INDIAN FOOD.

GOLDEN GOOSE?

I SAID SOME PEOPLE ARE *SPECIAL*, JIMMY. CADMUS' RESEARCH ONLY GOES AS FAR AS THE ABILITY TO CLONE THE *LIVING*.

YES, YOU/WE CAN FREEZE DNA--USE IT *LATER*, BUT IT *ISN'T* AS GOOD--IT ISN'T AS PERFECT. THE CLONES *DON'T* LAST--THEY LIVE A FEW YEARS THEN AGE AND DIE IN A FEW *MINUTES*.

HARPER WAS *UNIQUE*. THAT WAS THE PROBLEM, *FEW* PEOPLE ARE PERFECT. CLONING *ISN'T* AN ALL-COMERS THING.

ANYWAY, BY JONATHAN DREW BEING QUICK ON THE TRIGGER HE PUT THE PROJECT'S RESEARCH BACK BY *TEN YEARS*.

AT LEAST THE CLONE *WASN'T* COGNIZANT. CAN YOU IMAGINE WHAT SEEING YOUR OWN MURDER WOULD DO TO YOU?

FIND HIS *CLONE*, JIMMY.

I DON'T UNDERSTAND? *HIS* CLONE? THE GUARDIAN I'M *FAMILAR* WITH IS *DEAD*? OR A KID OR *WHAT*?

THIS IS THE THING-- THE MOST *IMPORTANT* THING TO UNDERSTAND--

--A *LOT* OF WHAT YOU'VE SEEN WAS A CLONE--NO, CLONES *PLURAL*--OF THAT *FIRST* CLONE.

FIRST CLONE? DUBBILEX, *WHAT* ARE YOU TALKING ABOUT?

"REMEMBER? BACK *WHEN*? THEN. *THAT* WAS THE CLONE JIM HARPER GAVE HIS LIFE TO SEE BUT *ONCE*.

"*THAT'S* THE HERO YOU *FIRST* ENCOUNTERED."

SINCE THEN THAT CLONE HAS BEEN *CLONED* HIMSELF.

SOMETIMES THESE "GUARDIANS" RECALL *EVERY- THING* FROM THE PAST.

SOMETIMES THEY HAVE THE PERSONALITY OF *HOUSEFLIES*.

BUT THEY *ALL* DIE WITHIN A YEAR.

THE *FIRST* CLONE. THE BEST, *PERFECT* ONE. HE FOUND OUT. HE WENT *AWAY.* FIND HIM, JIMMY--HE *KNOWS* THINGS EVEN I DON'T.

JEEZ! WHERE DO I LOOK?

I HEARD HIM SAY A NAME. A PLACE. *WARPATH.* GO THERE.

AND WHAT ABOUT *YOU?*

I'M FINE.

IT HITS ME. THE *TRUTH.* I HOPE *NOT,* BUT--

DUBBILEX, *WHY* IS THE FLOOR WET? WHERE IS THE *WATER* COMING FROM?

WHY DO YOU *ASSUME* IT'S WATER?

WHY DO YOU ASSUME MY BLOOD FLOWS *RED* LIKE YOURS?

THE TRUTH *IS--*

NO.

DREW'S *ALREADY* BEEN HERE, JIMMY.

YOU'VE BEEN TALKING TO A *DEAD* MAN.

AT LEAST *THAT'S* HOW I'D LIKE YOU TO REMEMBER ME. AS A *MAN.*

WILL YOU? WILL YOU DO ME THAT HONOR?

I DO SOME RESEARCH ON WARPATH.

(OH, AND WHEN I WAS READING STONE'S FILE--I WAS IN A MOTEL--NO DUMMY, ME. I DROVE BY MY APARTMENT. THE FIRE CREW WERE STILL PUTTING OUT THE FLAMES. YEAH, IF I OWNED ANYTHING I CARED ABOUT, I WOULD HAVE BEEN UPSET.)

SO, ANYWAY, I ADJOURNED TO THE LIBRARY AND INQUIRED ABOUT--

--WARPATH.

SOUTH--WAY SOUTH IN THE FINE, HOT STATE OF ARIZONA.

MORE FUGITIVES ARRESTED THERE THAN ANY OTHER TOWN/CITY (IT'S SOMEWHERE BETWEEN THE TWO--CAN'T MAKE UP ITS MIND WHICH IT IS.)

TO MAKE MATTERS WORSE--

--SUPER-VILLAINS. BAD GUYS GET SUPER-POWERS, WHY WOULDN'T YOU ASSUME THAT'S HAPPENING SOUTH OF THE BORDER, TOO? THEY CROSS THE BORDER FOR BETTER PAY JUST LIKE THE GARDENERS AND THE PICKERS OF PEACHES.

NO. THOSE THAT CAN FLY-- THEY FLY.

THOSE WHOSE POWERS, THOUGH MIGHTY--LIMIT THEM TO ONE FOOT IN FRONT OF THE NEXT--CROSS THE BORDER ILLEGALLY LIKE ANY IMMIGRANT WITHOUT THE PROPER PAPERS.

AND THEIR FIRST PORT OF CALL--

I FEEL HIM BEFORE I SEE HIM.

I ASK MYSELF--

--WHEN I HAVE A HEARTBEAT OF A MOMENT TO ASK MYSELF--

--IF I HEARD CORRECTLY-- WHAT I THINK I HEARD.

I HADN'T VANISHED.

IN THE FOYER OF STONE'S BUILDING THE DESK CLERK WAS GONE. HIS COUNTER WAS EMPTY--A GOOD PLACE TO HIDE AS DREW EMERGED AND SAID...

DREW CAN READ MINDS. DREW CAN SENSE MINDS AND THOUGHTS. BUT NOT MINE.

BLAM

BLAM

WHY CAN'T I READ YOUR MIND?

WHY?

I DON'T KNOW. BUT--

PIEW   PIEW

I THINK ABOUT WHERE I AM ON THE MAP. WHERE I'M NEAR.

I THINK OF THE RISK.

BLAM

BLAM

BLAM

PING

PIEW

PIEW

RISK, NO MATTER WHAT, **BEATS** THE CERTAIN DEATH THAT JONATHAN DREW PROMISES, SO--

I **TELL** MY BIKE WHAT I'M PLANNING.

BLAM

BLAM

"I **CAN'T** SWIM," MY BIKE SAYS BACK.

PIEW

PIEW

PIEW

"HELL, THE **FALL'LL** PROBABLY KILL US," I RESPOND.

BLAM

SO MY BIKE MAKES LIKE **SUNDANCE**--

--AND JIMMY OLSEN MAKES LIKE **NEWMAN**, AND I'M **COOLER** THAN THE JUSTICE LEAGUE AND THE DOOM PATROL AND METAL MEN COMBINED.

I THINK IT'S ALL I'VE BEEN THROUGH.

RED K. TURTLE OLSEN. ELASTIC OLSEN. I MEAN IT HAS TO BE.

MY BRAIN'S CHANGED WITH MY BODY EACH TIME AFTER TIME AFTER TIME AFTER TIME.

HOW ELSE COULD THIS SUPERHUMAN--

--FIEND--

--WHO READS MINDS AND BLOWS MINDS--

IF HE COULD READ MY MIND HE'D KNOW. HE'D KNOW. THAT I--

I RELAX. THE WATER'S COOL. I CAN BREATHE.

I WAIT FOR AN HOUR. NO, MORE THAN AN HOUR.

THEN I SURFACE.

THEN I DRY.

THEN I TRAVEL BY THUMB--

--TO WARPATH.

--LIKE NO OTHER TOWN.

IF DODGE CITY OF **OLD** AND KEYSTONE OF **NEW** HAD A CHILD, IT'D BE **THIS** PLACE.

PART OLD-WEST STYLE, PART MACHINE-AGE **WONDER** FROM FACTORIES USING DAY LABOR FROM THIS SIDE OF THE BORDER AND THE **OTHER** SIDE, TOO.

THE LAW-ABIDERS GO HOME-- TO **THIS** SIDE AND **THAT** AT THE END OF THE DAY.

WHEN I GET TO TOWN I FIND AN INTERNET CAFE. MUFFIN AND A REDEYE WAKE ME UP AND I GET BROWSING (THE WEB THAT IS) ABOUT THE LAW HERE--THE LAW THAT **CAME** AND SAW AND **TAMED** THIS PLACE LIKE IT WAS DODGE AND EARP OF OLD.

THERE'S A **LOT** TO READ ABOUT THE MAN WHO WEARS THE SHERIFF'S STAR IN WARPATH.

LOTS OF STORIES, LOTS OF **AMAZING** STORIES-- ABOUT A MAN WHO'S CHEATED TIME AND AGE AND TIME **AGAIN**.

GREG SAUNDERS.

HE WAS A MYSTERY MAN IN THE DAY.

LOTS OF MYSTERY MEN SINCE THEN AND TO BE HONEST, I **NEVER** UNDERSTOOD THE MYSTIQUE OF THIS ONE.

A COWBOY ON AN INDIAN (MOTORBIKE). TWO GUNS, TWO FISTS. YEAH, **SO?**

STILL, HE'D BEEN THROUGH A LOT--TIME TRAVEL, DEATH, REBIRTH--**STANDARD** FOR SOME WHO DON THE MASK AND CAPE AND COWL.

BUT *NOW* HERE HE WAS BEFORE ME--

--*YOUNG* AGAIN. WITH *BRIGHT* EYES, BUT *OLD, WISE* EYES, TOO.

--THE *ONLY* THING THAT BETRAYED THE LIFE AND YEARS HE'D LIVED.

OH, AND HIS SHERIFF'S STAR WAS *BIG* AND *BRIGHT.*

SO *WHAT* DO YOU WANT TO KNOW, MR. OLSEN?

JIMMY, SHERIFF SAUNDERS.

FINE. JIMMY. *WHAT'S* YOUR QUESTION?

ER, JAMES OR JIM HARPER. HE *CAME* HERE, HE'S *HERE.* AT LEAST I *HOPE* SO. MAN OF ACTION-- LIKE YOU.

YOU **DON'T** KNOW ME TO SAY THAT.

I READ. YOU HAVE A **HISTORY**.

HISTORY IS OFTEN BUT A **PATINA** OF REAL COME THE LIGHT OF TOMORROW.

CAN I **QUOTE** YOU ON THAT?

WHY?

IT'S A **GOOD** QUOTE.

I TRY TO KEEP A **QUIET**, SAFE TOWN. QUOTES AND THE LIKE BRING **ATTENTION** TO WARPATH--'FORE YOUR NEWSPAPER GOES FROM TODAY'S HEADLINES TO **TOMORROW'S** BIRD CAGE LINING.

I'VE BEEN AROUND LONG ENOUGH I KNOW THIS TO BE **TRUE**, AND--ON THAT YOU CAN QUOTE ME.

INDEED. SO. WARPATH? SAFE PLACE, **WASN'T** BEFORE. STILL, IT'S A MAYBE AND ALMOST WHEN IT COMES TO SUPER-VILLAINS IF YOU **DON'T** KEEP ON IT. **HOW** DID YOU, A SINGLE MAN, CHANGE ALL THAT?

I HAVE A **GOOD** TEAM BEHIND ME. PLUS I HAVE **IRON** WILL AND A BELIEF IN A **BETTER** TOMORROW.

YOU **HAVEN'T** ANSWERED MY QUESTION, BY THE WAY.

WHICH ONE, MR. OLSEN. YOU'VE ASKED A WHOLE PASSEL.

JAMES HARPER. HAVE YOU **ENCOUNTERED** SUCH A MAN?

--OF **ACTION**? NO, SIR. 'NFACT I SEE A MAN SUCH AS THAT TYPE, I TELL'EM TO **KEEP** MOVING ON. WAR-PATH **AIN'T** THE PLACE FOR ACTION NOR NONE OF THAT--NOT NO MORE.

ALL RIGHT, **ANOTHER** QUESTION.

YOUR **LAST**, MR. OLSEN. I HAVE MY **DUTIES** AND TIME TAKES THEM.

HOW DO YOU DO

IT?

THE **LAW**? CHANGE A **MAGNET** OF LAWLESSNESS INTO A PLACE WHERE PEOPLE AT LEAST FEEL **SOME** SAFETY?

I'M **HARD** AND FAIR. MY DEPUTIES--MY MEN AND WOMEN--I SAID, SORT'A--THEY ACT **ACCORDINGLY.**

BUT **HOW** DO YOU KEEP THE PLACE LOCKED DOWN DAY AND NIGHT?

DAYTIME THE COPS **DO** WHAT NEEDS DOING.

AND **NIGHT?**

I KEEP MY EYES **OPEN.**

IN OTHER WORDS YOU STAY ALERT? THAT **DOESN'T** SEEM ENOUGH.

IN OTHER WORDS--**YOUR** WORDS--ALERT, **NO.** BUT **COMES** THE NIGHTTIME--

BLAM

BLAM BLAM

BLAM

I HAD SOME MONEY *STASHED* IN MY SHORTS. ONCE IT DRIED OUT, I USED IT--TO BUY *INFORMATION*.

A *LOCAL* IMPORTER OF SOUTH AMERICAN TALENT--AS IN SUPER-VILLAINS--AS IN A SERIES OF BANK-RAIDS *NORTH* OF THE BORDER.

THE IMPORTER--ONE *JAMES WEDAA*--HIS DOMESTIC HELP NEEDS *VETTING*--FIFTY BUCKS AND I KNEW *EVERYTHING*.

SO I'M *HERE*. I'M *WATCHING*. I'M--

SAUNDERS, IS--

GET HIM, YOU NIMRODS!

HE'S BUT ONE MAN.

--WOEFULLY OUTNUMBERED.

BLAM

FWOOSH

BLAM BLAM

BLAM BLAM

HE'S FANTASTIC, BUT--

--THERE ARE SO MANY.

WHAT SHOULD I DO? WHAT COULD ANYONE D--

KRAK

THUD

AT FIRST I DON'T RECOGNIZE--I DON'T KNOW WHAT I'M WATCHING.

WHO.

AND THEN THE SHIELD TELLS ME.

I WATCH TWO MEN BEAT AN ARMY.

KRAK

IT MIGHT BE THE MOST AMAZING THING I'VE EVER SEEN.

I LEAVE SAUNDERS TO MOP UP THE MESS.

I FOLLOW HIS SAVIOR.

I'M SCARED. HE SEEMS SO DIFFERENT FROM THE MAN I KNEW. CRAZY.

PLUS, THERE'S SOMETHING OUT THERE. A CREATURE. A DOG OR--

NO.

I'VE COME THIS FAR.

I'VE COME TOO FAR TO QUIT.

WHAT DO YOU WANT, OLSEN?

OH. *HI.* HELLO. MR. HARPER. JAMES. *JIM.*

YOU *REMEMBER* ME?

I'VE GOT EYES AND MEMORY, BOY. IT'S *NOT* THAT HARD.

HOW DID YOU FIND ME?

I LOOKED, MR. HARPER. IT *WASN'T* EASY. IN FACT I'M KIND OF *PROUD* OF MYSELF THAT I DID--

AND I'M *MAD* AS HELL THAT YOU DID, YOU LITTLE *SNOOP.* YOU KNOW, I *NEVER* DID TRUST YOU.

I'M *SORRY* TO HEAR THAT, MR. HARPER, BUT--

ER--DO YOU HAVE A *PET?* A DOG OR A MONKEY OR--

--I JUST GET THE FEELING THERE'S *SOMETHING* OUT THERE AND IT'S CREEPING THE *BEJEEZUS* OUT OF ME.

NOT A MONKEY BUT *CLOSE.* MY DAUGHTER.

FIVE HOURS LATER

THE CAR RENTAL **MAXES** OUT MY **MASTERCARD,** BUT I **CAN'T** THINK ABOUT IT NOW.

I HAVE TO GET BACK.

SO **MANY** HAVE **DIED** SO OTHERS MIGHT CLOSE THE **BOOK** ON THE **TRUTH**--SO **MANY** THAT DREW HAS **KILLED**--

I HAVE TO MAKE IT **HOME.** METROPOLIS.

I HAVE TO GET THERE--TELL **SOMEONE**--

--THEY'RE GOING TO KILL SUPERMAN.

I'M SUPERMAN'S **PAL,** AND I'LL SEE THIS **THROUGH** FOR THE SAKE OF THE TRUTH AND THE DEAD AND MY FRIEND WHO MEANS **MORE** TO ME THAN ANYTHING.

YEAH. NO SELF-DOUBT. NO "CAN I, CAN'T I?".

I WILL.

OR MY NAME ISN'T JIMMY OLSEN.

I SEE HIM.

I SEE OLSEN.

I KNOW *WHO* HE IS-- OLSEN--SNOOPING *DAMN* OLSEN--

--BY THE GLINT OF HIS RED HAIR IN THE MORNING'S GLOW.

I LOOKED, MR. HARPER. IT *WASN'T* EASY. IN FACT I'M KIND OF *PROUD* OF MYSELF THAT I DID--

OLSEN. OF COURSE. IT *HAD* TO BE HIM.

I HAVE QUESTIONS, MR. HARPER.

SO.

AS WE TALK.

AS I STALL.

I THINK. I ASK MYSELF.

ABOUT THE NEWSBOYS. ABOUT CADMUS. ABOUT A MAN NAMED DREW.

AND WHY YOU RAN.

DO I LIE?

DO I TELL THE *TRUTH*?

LIES?

TRUTH?

I GUESS I'LL *START* AT THE BEGINNING...

WARNING, PRIVATE PROPERTY, ALL TRANSGRESSORS WILL BE MET WITH ARMED RESPONSE

CADMUS FACILITY DELTA, SALEM. TIMES PAST.

EDDY.

YES, RON.

I FEAR I AM IN THE *MIDST* OF AN EXISTENTIAL CRISIS.

I WONDER *WHY* I AM HERE.

HOWSO?

ON EARTH OR IN CADMUS, RON?

BOTH. ONE. THE OTHER. BOTH.

I MEAN, WE'RE HIGH-TECH *POWER* GUYS. GOD HELP THE FELLOW WHO TRIES TO *CROSS* US. AND FOR *WHAT?* WE GUARD THIS DOOR TO D-WING.

D-WING. WHAT OR WHERE OR *WHY* FOR THAT MATTER--ARE A, B AND C-WINGS? *NOT* IN SUNNY SALEM.

WE WAIT AND *WASTE* OUR DAYS.

I HEAR YOU, RON, BUT--

AND FOR *WHAT?* WE DON'T EVEN *KNOW* WHAT'S ON THE OTHER SIDE OF THAT DOOR.

AND FROM *WHAT* I CAN SEE--

--NO ONE CARES *ENOUGH* TO FIND OUT.

"SO WHAT WAS IT? WHAT DID YOU SEE?"

"ER, HONESTLY, OLSEN..."

HMM

REMEMBER, CADMUS HAS GENETICALLY CREATED *ALL* MANNER OF WILD CREATURES.

THIS ONE WAS *DIFFERENT*, THOUGH.

HOW SO?

"WELL, FOR *ONE THING*...

"...IT WORE A RING."

NOW I'M *NO FOLLOWER* OF FASHION, JIMMY, BUT AS FAR AS I RECALL, *NONE* OF CADMUS' MONSTROSITIES CAME WEARING COSTUME JEWELRY.

SO *WHAT* DID YOU DO NEXT?

NOTHING.

"IT TOLD ME NOT TO."

"*TELEPATHICALLY.* IT SPOKE TO ME."

DO NOT WORRY.

DO NOT DO.

I WILL BE FINE.

THE SCIENCE POLICE WILL COME.

WELL *GOOD LUCK* TO YOU, FRIEND.

YES. FRIEND.

WHOA. *WHOA*, MR. HARPER.

YOU CALLED ME JIM *ONCE* UPON A TIME.

AND YOU CALLED ME *JIMMY*. NOW I'M OLSEN?

ALL RIGHT, JIMMY, *WHY* THE "WHOA"?

YOU *BEGIN* THE BEGUINE IN SALEM? I *DIDN'T* EVEN KNOW CADMUS HAD A PLACE THERE. SALEM IS DR. FATE--*MAGIC*-- ALL THAT.

AND WHERE *BETTER* TO HIDE A PLACE OF SCIENCE.

MONSTERS OR ALIENS OR I-*DON'T*-KNOW-WHAT-NOR-YOU-WHAT. THAT'S *CRAZY*.

YEAH. I'M *NOT* ARGUING THAT POINT. *NOR* THAT I STARTED THIS AT THE *WRONG* PLACE. THE START--WAS--WELL--

I WAS HAVING PROBLEMS *SLEEPING*. MEMORIES *NOTHING* SOLID AND BRIGHT. SHARDS.

SOME MINE. SOME MY *FATHER'S*.

FATHER?

THE GENU BEER CHAR

Voll-D

DOBLE MALT

THE MAN I WAS CLONED FROM. THE *ORIGINAL* JIM HARPER. THE ORIGINAL *GUARDIAN.* CALLING HIM MY FATHER ALLOWS ME THE *PATINA*--YOU MIGHT ARGUE THE *DELUSION*--OF MY OWN HUMANITY.

ANYWAY, I WAS *TROUBLED* BY WHAT I COULDN'T REMEMBER AND WHAT I *COULD.*

"I SOUGHT HELP."

WHY ARE YOU HERE, MR. HARPER?

YOU WERE RECOMMENDED-- *HIGHLY*--FOR MEMORIES.

IT'S CONSIDERED MY *FORTE,* I ADMIT.

WELL, I HAVE A PROBLEM WITH MEMORY-- MINE.

MR. HARPER, *MAY* I ASK YOU...

...HAVE YOU EVER BEEN HYPNOTIZED?

69

THIRTY-SEVEN MINUTES LATER.

I'M *SORRY*, DOCTOR. OF COURSE I'LL MAKE *RESTITUTION* FOR ALL OF THIS.

SO WHAT HAPPENED?

I *REMEMBERED*.

WHAT EXACTLY?

OH, WHAT I *DID* AND *DIDN'T* DO. AND--

"--I REMEMBERED MY FATHER."

I *HAD* TO SEE HIM.

WELL NOW YOU HAVE, IT'S THE *LAST* THING YOU WILL.

AREN'T I TOO IMPORTANT TO ALL THIS?

I HAVE MY *ORDERS*. NO ONE SEES THIS AND *LIVES*-- AT LEAST THOSE WITHOUT THE RIGHT LEVEL OF CLEARANCE. SO--

YOU *STILL* THINK IT WAS WORTH IT?

JUST DO WHAT YOU HAVE TO DO AND WE CAN BOTH BE ON OUR WAY.

SO YOUR *FIRST* MEMORY--

YEAH, THE *DEATH* OF MY FATHER.

AND *DREW.*

WHAT?

JONATHAN DREW, CODENAME: *ASSASSIN.* HE MUST BE A PART OF THAT MEMORY, *TOO*--YOUR DAD'S KILLER AND ALL.

THE *ONE* PIECE OF INFORMATION I *COULDN'T* UNCOVER. AND *YET* BY WAITING HERE, IT *COMES* TO ME.

AS I HOPE *HE* DOES--THIS DREW GUY. *THAT'S* WHY I'M HERE, INCIDENTALLY. I'M *WAITING* FOR HIM.

I ASSUMED HE'D BE *ALONG* BY NOW, TRUTH BE TOLD.

NO OFFENSE, JIMMY, BUT IF *YOU* FOUND ME, I FIGURE HE'D HAVE SHOWN UP *LONG* BEFORE NOW.

IT'S NOT LIKE I'VE DONE SO GREAT A JOB OF HIDING.

I WANT TO LOOK *INTO* THE FACE OF THE MAN WHO KILLED MY DAD ONE LAST TIME BEFORE I TAKE MY REVENGE.

REVENGE? AS IN KILLING? THAT *DOESN'T* SOUND LIKE YOU.

LIKE *WHO?* WHO AM I?

THE *MORE* I'VE LEARNED, THE MORE I *ASK* THAT QUESTION OF MYSELF, JIMMY. SPECTRE, DR. FATE, HAWKMAN AND HIS MANY LIVES--IT *ALL* TELLS ME THERE'S SOME FORM OF *AFTERLIFE.*

SOULS. *YOU* HAVE ONE. SO, I PRESUME, DOES JIM HARPER, MY FATHER, AND IT/HE *ABIDES* WHEREVER SOULS ABIDE AFTER THE BODY DIES.

BUT WHAT ABOUT *ME?* AM I A MAN OR A *THING?* IS A CLONE A HUMAN IN ITS OWN RIGHT? I WALK THROUGH THE WORLD WITH ANOTHER MAN'S MEMORIES. *HOW* CAN I DARE SAY I AM MY OWN ENTITY?

I DON'T KNOW WHAT TO SAY.

AND *I'M* JUST TALKING MORE FOR THE SAKE OF IT THAN--*ANYWAY,* WHERE WERE WE--

THAT TOLD ME TO *KEEP* INVESTIGATING. IT WAS HANDY BEING THE GUARDIAN OF CADMUS *THEN.* I COULD LOOK, AND *NOBODY* LOOKED BACK AT ME--ALL BRIGHT AND SHINING GOLD AND HIDING THERE IN PLAIN SIGHT.

A BIG OL'YELLOW, BLACK-EYED MONSTER.

YEAH, WITH A RING. FITTED HIM/HER/IT LIKE'D BEEN *MEASURED* FOR IT, TOO.

TOLD ME CADMUS HAD SOME *HINKY* DEALINGS GOING ON IN THE SHADOWS.

"SO I *PEERED.*

"PROWLED."

"DE-ENCRYPTED."

AND *WHAT* DID YOU GET?

ULTIMATELY, JIMMY--

--THE *WORST* NIGHT OF MY LIFE.

"WHAT ELSE DID YOU FIND, JIMMY? WHAT-ALL ELSE DO YOU KNOW?"

"DO YOU KNOW OF A CADMUS FACILITY IN TWIN CITIES?"

"ER, CAN'T SAY I DO."

"NEITHER DID I UNTIL I LOOKED FOR IT.

"DID YOU KNOW SOME PEOPLE ARE SPECIAL? SOME PEOPLE ARE CLONE-WORTHY AND SOME NOT."

"JIM HARPER-- THE ORIGINAL-- I MEAN YOUR FATHER --YEAH. DUBBILEX SAID THAT."

"AND PAUL KIRK.

"A FEW OTHERS."

"WHAT ABOUT THE YOUNG NEWSBOYS--I MEAN THE ONES I HUNG WITH BACK IN THE CRAZY DAYS OF US AND YOU?"

"THEY COULD BE ALIVE AND WELL AND SOME-WHERE NOT HERE. THEY COULD BE PIECES IN TEST TUBES THE MILITARY STUDY EVERY CHRISTMAS. I DON'T KNOW.

"WHAT I **DO** KNOW-- WHAT I **LEARNED** FROM ALL THIS--

"--THERE IS A MILITARY OPERATION **READYING** ITSELF FOR ONE GOAL.

"THE **DEATH** OF SUPERMAN.

"THEY--THIS OPERATION--I **DON'T** KNOW THE FULL CATALOGUE OF HORROR THEY'VE **AMASSED** TO DO IT--

enter password: 619

"--OH, I KNOW **ENOUGH** NOW TO BE IMPRESSED--

"--BUT **MOSTLY** WHAT I KNOW--

"--IS THE **HORROR** THAT INVOLVED JIM HARPER. I TOOK **ONE** LOOK--

"THEY WANTED AN *ARMY*--A CLONE ARMY-- IT'S A GOOD IDEA IN SCIENCE FICTION MOVIES, BUT IN *REALITY* IT REQUIRES--

"--*MAD* SCIENCE.

"MY CELLS-- IMPERFECT CELLS OF A SOULLESS COPY--SPLICED WITH--*PAUL KIRK*-- COUNCIL SCIENCE--

"--I *DON'T KNOW* WHO THOUGHT THAT WAS A GOOD IDEA--AT THE TIME--

"--BUT AT *THIS* TIME--

"--I SAW A *BOSCH* PAINTING OF MY ALTERNATIVE EXISTENCES, NONE OF THEM BEING *ANYTHING* BUT VILE AND SICK AND AN INSULT TO THE MEMORY OF THE FIRST JIM HARPER AND PAUL KIRK, *TOO*, FOR THAT MATTER."

SO *WHAT* DID YOU *DO?*

WHAT DID PAUL KIRK *DO?* HE TOOK *BACK* HIS HUMANITY.

NOW AS I SAID--I'M *NOT* SURE I HAVE THAT TO BEGIN WITH, *BUT* I FELT I OWED MY FATHER HIS. AND *SO*--

"YOU KILLED THEM *ALL*?"

I'M *NOT* SURE THEY WERE ALIVE TO *BEGIN* WITH.

BUT YEAH, -- I *GUESS* -- YEAH, I DID.

"I KILLED THEM ALL."

IS **THIS** WHAT YOU WANTED TO HEAR, JIMMY?

IS THIS WHAT YOU WANTED TO **KNOW**?

THE GUARDIAN-- JIM HARPER'S **LEGACY**-- IS A **STEW** OF FALSEHOODS. I DID MAYBE **HALF** OF THE DEEDS I'M CREDITED WITH. THE **REST** WERE DONE BY **FAULTY** COPIES OF ME--AND ME MYSELF A COPY OF A DEAD MAN.

A MAN KILLED BY DREW. **JONATHAN DREW.** THAT'S A NAME I'VE BEEN **WAITING** TO LEARN FOR THE **WHOLE** WRETCHED SPAN OF MY EXISTENCE, SO I **THANK** YOU FOR THAT.

BUT **HAVE** I HELPED YOU?

NOW I **DEFINITELY** KNOW THERE'S SOMETHING AFOOT. THE **MILITARY.** BLACK BAG.

WHAT I **DON'T** KNOW IS WHY THEY WANT TO KILL SUPERMAN IN THE FIRST PLACE.

YEAH. BUT AT LEAST UNCOVERING **THIS** MUCH, I HAVE A START.

YEAH. **SURE.** A START.

CLONES. **NOT** ME, BUT A **CADRE** OF CLONES. AND MAGIC. AND KRYPTONITE. **AND** THE AUTHORITY TO PAROLE ALL MANNER OF EVIL. BLACK BAG, SON--THEY GOT A **WHOLE** LOT OF BAGS **FULL** OF ALL MANNER OF I DON'T KNOW.

OH, AND IF THIS OP HAS A NAME, I DIDN'T LEARN IT, BUT I DID DIG UP THAT IT HAS A NUMBER. **SIGNIFICANCE?** YOU GOT ME. BUT THE NUMBER IS **7734.**

"YOU KILLED THEM ALL?"

"I'M NOT SURE THEY WERE ALIVE TO BEGIN WITH."

"BUT YEAH,-- I GUESS-- YEAH, I DID."

"I KILLED THEM ALL."

GWENDOLINE. CLEAN UP. PACK UP.

IT'S *TIME* I SHOWED YOU THE CITY.

WHAT ABOUT *YOU*, DADDY? YOU DON'T SMELL SO GOOD.

AND *YOU* ARE A RUDE AND *WILLFUL* GIRL, BUT YEAH, I GUESS I *COULD* DO WITH A SCRUB AND SCRAPE--

"--I GUESS."

PAPA?

YEAH, GIRL.

WHERE ARE WE GOING?

FAR FROM HERE, FAR TO THERE, FAR.

NOT *MUCH* OF AN ANSWER, PAPA. I HATE IT WHEN YOU'RE CRYPTIC.

OH YOU DO, DO YOU? WHEN I'M CRYPTIC? WHERE'D YOU EVEN LEARN THAT WORD?

FROM YOUR DVDS OF OLD TV SHOWS. BANACEK. *HE* WAS CRYPTIC ALL THE TIME.

PEPPARD. HE'S *COOL*. NOT McQUEEN, BUT--

HE REMINDS ME OF *YOU*, PAPA. PEPPARD, I MEAN.

THANK YOU, GIRL. I'LL TAKE THAT AS A *COMPLIMENT*.

HEY, I FOUND THIS IN THE BACK OF THE TRUCK. WHAT IS IT?

TROPHY. SHINY AND *NOT* WORTH MUCH ELSE, LIKE MOST TROPHIES ARE.

SO I SHOULD DO *WHAT* WITH IT? THROW IT *AWAY*?

SURE, WHY NOT.

NO. HOLD ON TO IT.

LOOKS LIKE I *MIGHT* NEED IT YET.

WELL, *HERE* WE ARE, GIRL. THE CITY.

PAPA, I GOTTA SAY-- I'M A LITTLE *SCARED.*

YEAH, ME TOO. I *CONFESS* THIS *WASN'T* WHAT I WAS EXPECTING.

STILL AND ALL, IT *DON'T* MATTER--

83

JONATHAN KENT

BELOVED HUSBAND
AND FATHER

"We were put on this
Earth for a reason, but it's
up to us to find it."

CLARK?

CLARK?
ARE YOU OKAY?

NO.

BRAINIAC'S STILL ALIVE AND MY FATHER'S NOT.

YOU CAN'T THINK THAT WAY.

MY FATHER'S DEAD, LOIS, AND THERE'S NOTHING I CAN DO.

YES, THERE IS.

NEVER FORGET WHAT HE TAUGHT YOU.

...IF THERE *ARE* PEOPLE THAT NEED HELP, YOU DO WHAT YOU ALWAYS DO.

DON'T LET *ANYONE* OR *ANYTHING* GET IN YOUR WAY.

I WON'T.

FOR THE CHEST.

...IF THERE *ARE* PEOPLE THAT NEED HELP, YOU DO WHAT YOU ALWAYS DO.

DON'T LET *ANYONE* OR *ANYTHING* GET IN YOUR WAY.

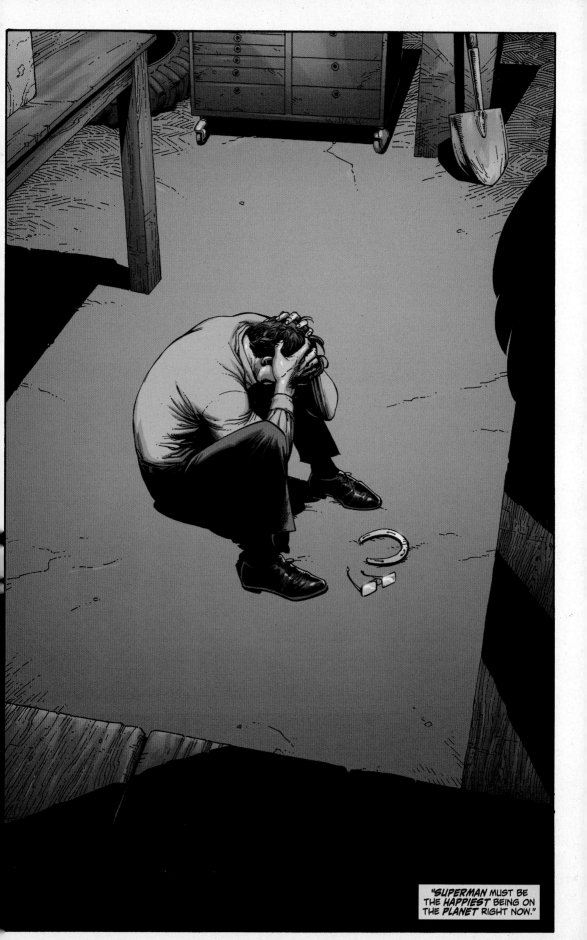

"*SUPERMAN* MUST BE THE *HAPPIEST* BEING ON THE *PLANET* RIGHT NOW."

HE JUST RESCUED AN ESTIMATED *ONE HUNDRED THOUSAND* KRYPTONIANS FROM BRAINIAC.

WE DON'T HAVE A VISUAL ON SUPERMAN ANYWHERE NEAR THE FORTRESS OR THE KRYPTONIAN CITY THAT *EXPANDED* NEXT TO IT.

THE SKIES ARE STILL *CLEAR* OVER KANDOR.

BUT FOR HOW *LONG,* AGENT ASSASSIN?

HOW LONG UNTIL THOSE BEINGS DEVELOP THE POWERS *SUPERMAN* HAS?

HOW LONG UNTIL THEY DECIDE TO VENTURE *OUTSIDE* OF KANDOR?

I'VE HAD A VESTED INTEREST IN THE MAN OF STEEL FOR *YEARS.* I'VE BEEN FORCED TO ACCEPT HIM AS EVERYONE ELSE HAS. AS A VISITOR WHO'S MADE EARTH HIS HOME.

TECHNICALLY, HE'S DONE A GREAT *MANY* THINGS FOR THIS COUNTRY.

BUT THIS COULD CHANGE HIS PRIORITIES, SIR.

THIS *WILL* CHANGE THEM.

GENTLEMEN...

MA...

...I'M SORRY I COULDN'T SAVE HIM.

YOU HAVE ABSOLUTELY NOTHING TO BE SORRY FOR, CLARK. DO YOU UNDERSTAND ME?

NOTHING.

NOW YOU GO. YOU GO DO YOUR JOB. RIGHT THIS SECOND.

I DON'T KNOW HOW MUCH BETTER THIS CAN GET. THE DIVERSITY IN ARCHITECTURE--

IT REFLECTS THE DIFFERENT GUILDS OF KRYPTON, KAL. OUR HOUSE, THE HOUSE OF EL, IS ONE OF MANY AMONG THE SCIENCE GUILD.

THE SOLDIER'S GUILD IS REPRESENTED BY THOSE BUNKER-LIKE FORMATIONS. THE HOUSE OF ZOD BELONGS TO THEM--

ZOD?

GENERAL ZOD IS STILL CONSIDERED A *HERO* BY MANY FOR HIS VALIANT BATTLE AGAINST BRAINIAC.

MANY OF THE SOLDIERS HE LED AGAINST THE COLUAN INVADER WERE ABDUCTED ALONG WITH THE REST OF US.

IT'S TRAGIC TO LEARN OF ZOD'S FATE. AND WORSE YET, NON.

NON WAS A WONDERFUL MENTOR TO YOUR FATHER. AND TO *US*.

UNFORTUNATELY, ZOD'S CRIMES DIDN'T *END* WITH HIS TURN AGAINST MY FATHER.

HE RECENTLY *ESCAPED* THE *PHANTOM ZONE* AND DECIMATED METROPOLIS. BECAUSE OF THAT, THERE'LL BE SOME ON EARTH WHO WON'T *TRUST* YOU.

BUT I WANT TO SHOW THEM THAT THEY CAN. I WANT TO BRING THEM HERE.

THIS IS WHY I WANT YOU TO MEET THE PEOPLE OF EARTH. SO THAT THEY CAN TEACH YOU THE RULES HERE.

I'VE HAD A LIFETIME TO LEARN THEM, AND KARA'S HAD ME.

WE NEED TO TEACH THOSE RULES TO THE PEOPLE OF KRYPTON.

I SEE YOUR POINT, KAL. BUT--

--ALURA AND I MAY BE IN CHARGE OF THE CITY, BUT WE DON'T *CONTROL* THEM.

THE *OLD* COUNCIL TRIED TO *SILENCE* MY BROTHER, AND WE LOST KRYPTON FOREVER BECAUSE OF IT. HERE, EVERYONE IS *FREE* TO DO AS THEY PLEASE.

AND JUDGING FROM WHERE I'M STANDING, THEY PLEASE TO GO INSTEAD OF WAITING FOR PEOPLE OF EARTH TO COME.

THEY MUST BE SUPERVISED.

THEY'LL BE *CAREFUL.*

WHAT IS IT, JIMMY? YOU CAN TALK TO ME.

DO YOU REMEMBER THE MAN ON THE ROOF WHEN SUPES FOUGHT ATLAS?

I REMEMBER YOU KEPT SEEING SOMETHING UP THERE. I MISSED IT EVERY TIME I LOOKED UP.

WELL, I GOT ONE PHOTO AND I I.D.ED THE GUY. CLARK SAID I SHOULD FOLLOW THE TRAIL AND BE THE REPORTER I WANTED TO BE, AND I LISTENED, AND I DID WHAT HE SUGGESTED--THAT'S WHY I'VE BEEN AWAY. YEAH, I FOLLOWED THE TRAIL--

--FROM CADMUS INTO THE DESERT. DID YOU EVER HEAR OF A PLACE CALLED WARPATH?

CLOSE TO THE MEXICAN BORDER?

YEAH, CRAZY PLACE. BUT I MET MEN THERE. REAL MEN. I ESCAPED DEATH, TOO. COUPLE OF TIMES.

O RIO, SEGUNDO INF

YOU **DON'T** UNDERSTAND, I--

OH, I **UNDERSTAND**-- I **UNDERSTAND** THAT YOU ARE **NOT** A SPORTSWRITER TODAY, YOU GOT ME?

YOU **ARE** COVERING THIS EVENT LIKE **EVERYONE** ELSE.

PERRY, DARLING.

AND THAT GOES FOR **YOU** TOO, CAT. NO SOCIETY PAGE TODAY. NO OPINION PAGE.

BUT I JUST UNCOVERED A **JUICY**--

CAT! EARTH'S POPULATION HAS **JUST** INCREASED BY THE **SUM** OF ONE HUNDRED THOUSAND KRYPTONIANS.

AND **JUDGING** FROM THE TELEVISION REPORTS, **NONE** OF THEM ARE VERY **SHY**, APPARENTLY.

IF THIS ISN'T "**JUICY**," I DON'T KNOW WHAT IS.

PERRY...

I **DON'T** CARE **WHICH** TEAM YOU THINK WILL MAKE THE PLAYOFFS, LOMBARD.

...I **JUST** GOT WORD FROM SUPERMAN. AND YOU WON'T BELIEVE--

HE'S BRINGING A KRYPTONIAN **DELEGATION** TO METROPOLIS-- TO MEET THE **PRESIDENT.**

WAIT? NOT DC? GREAT CAESAR'S GHOST!

METROPOLIS IS HIS HOME ON **EARTH.** HE FEELS A GOOD **FIRST** STEP WILL BE THE PEOPLE OF HIS **OLD** WORLD MEETING THE **LEADER** OF THE COUNTRY IN THE PLACE HE LIVES, IN THE HERE AND NOW.

HE'S ON HIS WAY TO ANTARCTICA AT **THIS MOMENT** TO ESCORT THEM BACK **HERE.**

I WANT YOU THERE--HERE, I MEAN--METROPOLIS, NOT THE NORTH POLE, ALTHOUGH YOU MIGHT BE GOING THERE **TOO** IF THIS STORY GETS ANY BIGGER.

OOH.

NO **OOH.** THIS STORY IS THE **ONLY** STORY. NOW. **FIRST.** NOW.

OLSEN, YOU TOO. NOW.

I'M ON IT, CHIEF.

DON'T CALL ME CHIEF.

OH AND LOIS...

...WHERE'S CLARK?

ER, *WRAPPING* UP SOME STUFF WITH HIS FAMILY. YOU KNOW. IT'S A *TOUGH* TIME FOR HIM AT THE MOMENT.

HE SAID HE'D BE BACK HERE *TOMORROW* AT THE LATEST.

I GUESS I CAN LIVE WITH THAT.

STILL-- *HELL* OF A TIME--

YEAH, CLARK'S SORRY, PERRY.

NO. I MEAN THIS-- ALL THIS--IS *ONE HELL OF A TIME!*

NOW GO!

YOU, AS *YOU'RE* AWARE, AS *WE* ARE AWARE, ARE THE MOST *POWERFUL* BEING ON THE PLANET.

I SUP-POSE.

AT LEAST YOU *WERE*. NOW YOU'RE ONE OF HOW *MANY*?

I HAVEN'T DONE A HEAD COUNT.

NEWS REPORTERS SEEM TO HAVE A NUMBER IN MIND, BUT LET'S JUST SAY A *WHOLE* HECK OF A LOT, THEN.

A HUNDRED THOUSAND "*YOUS*" FLYING AROUND BEING SUPER AND STRONG AND *ALL* THAT YOU ARE.

ABOUT A HUNDRED THOUSAND.

THEY *WON'T*. THE GROUP YOU SPOKE OF WERE ESCAPED WAR CRIMINALS FROM THE PHANTOM ZONE LED BY ZOD.

THESE PEOPLE-- KANDORIANS. AFTER *ALL* THEY'VE BEEN THROUGH WITH *BRAINIAC*--ALL THEY WANT IS THE *THINGS* WE ALL WANT--PEACE AND FREEDOM.

THEY *KNOW* THEY'RE GUESTS HERE.

EXCEPT THEY'RE *NOT* YOU, ARE THEY, KAL?

NO MORE THAN *I* AM JUST AN AMAZON OR *KENDRA* IS JUST A THANAGARIAN.

ACTUALLY, DI, I'M *NOT* A THANAGARIAN AT ALL.

OH. YES. FORGIVE ME.

NEVER-THELESS, KAL, YOU *GET* DIANA'S POINT.

TWENTY-*SEVEN* OF YOUR RACE *ALMOST* DESTROYED METROPOLIS NOT LONG AGO.

IMAGINE WHAT A HUNDRED THOUSAND OF YOU COULD DO.

...EARTH WILL BE A *BETTER* PLACE FOR ALL THAT'S HAPPEN-ING *NOW*.

LOOK, LEAVE *EVERYTHING* TO ME. I THINK THE *SOLUTION* IS THAT AMERICA NEEDS TO RECOGNIZE KANDOR OR NEW KRYPTON OR WHATEVER IT ENDS UP CALLING ITSELF. IT WILL BE A GOOD FIRST STEP THAT THE WHOLE WORLD WILL SIT UP AND TAKE NOTICE OF. AND FROM *THERE*...

...I'LL ORGANIZE *TEACHERS* TO VISIT THEM-- *SHOW* THEM THE WAYS OF EARTH.

THESE PEOPLE WILL *LEARN* ABOUT KRYPTON IN TURN AND *BOTH* OF MY RACES WILL GET SOMETHING OUT OF THIS.

LOOK, BOTTOM LINE, GUYS, I *PROMISE* YOU THIS...

ZOR-EL.

KAL! HELLO.

ARE YOU *READY*? I'M SORRY TO RUSH YOU, *BUT*--THE EYES OF THE WORLD ARE UPON US.

YES, YES. WE--I--AM JUST *WAITING* FOR--

--AHH, *THERE* SHE IS.

I *MADE* IT, FATHER. MOTHER.

KARA, I **WASN'T** EXPECTING YOU.

PERHAPS BECAUSE YOU **DIDN'T** ASK ME.

AND I'M **SURE** KAL HAS HIS REASONS, DAUGHTER.

YES, THE PRESIDENT'S **PLANE**--AIR FORCE ONE--KARA MADE IT CRASH. SHE'S **NOT** A POPULAR FIGURE WHERE WE'RE GOING.

YOU SEE, KAL HAS A POINT. **PERHAPS** YOU SHOULD--

SHE'S OUR **DAUGHTER**, ALURA. WE'RE A FAMILY-- AGAIN, **FINALLY**. SHE FLIES WITH US.

SO BE IT.

ANYONE **ELSE** I SHOULD MEET BEFORE WE GO?

THIS IS OUR **CHIEF OF SECURITY**.

THARA AK-VAR.

THARA? THARA! FINALLY!

I'VE BEEN ASKING **EVERYONE** WHERE YOU **WERE**.

THEY'RE OLD FRIENDS, KAL.

I WAS *BUSY* ORGANIZING-- TRAINING YOUR PARENTS' GUARD. I DIDN'T *MEAN* TO STAY AWAY.

WELL YOU'RE HERE *NOW*.

AND YOU-- CHIEF OF SECURITY. I *CAN'T* BELIEVE YOU WERE *GIVEN* SUCH AN IMPORTANT ROLE.

NO ONE GAVE ME ANYTHING. I *EARNED* IT.

YOU CAN CATCH UP *LATER*, GIRLS.

TIME DOESN'T WAIT--FOR MAN *OR* SUPERMAN. WE HAVE TO FLY.

THEN *LEAD ON*, KAL.

SHOW US YOUR WORLD!

141

IT FEELS *STRANGE*, DOESN'T IT?

AND WHAT WOULD *THAT* BE, MISTER PRESIDENT?

KNOWING YOU'VE JUST MADE *HISTORY*.

OH, AND MY PEOPLE INFORM ME SUPERGIRL IS YOUR *DAUGHTER*.

YES, THAT'S *CORRECT*.

THEN YOU *OWE* ME A PLANE. A REAL *BIG* ONE.

I'M JOKING.

NO!

NEW YORK.

I HAVE NO DOUBT OUR GENERAL TRIED TO CONVINCE THE COUNCIL TO PURSUE INTERSTELLAR TRAVEL SO HE COULD *HUNT* THIS COLUAN DOWN.

WE *HAVE* BRAINIAC'S *SHIP* UNDER STUDY, BUT THE HUMANS HAVE TAKEN THE ALIEN INTO CUSTODY.

THIS IS OUR CHANCE TO *AVENGE* KRYPTON. INSTEAD, KAL-EL WANTS TO PLAY *DIPLOMAT*.

ZOD MAY HAVE BEEN AT ODDS WITH THE COUNCIL MORE OFTEN THAN NOT, BUT HIS *LOYALTY* TO OUR WORLD AND ITS PEOPLE COULD *NEVER* BE QUESTIONED.

AND YET, THE SON OF JOR-EL CLAIMS ZOD COMMITTED HERESY AND MURDER *WITHOUT* JUSTIFICATION AFTER KANDOR'S DISAPPEARANCE.

DO YOU RECALL THE LAST WORDS GENERAL ZOD SAID TO US BEFORE WE WERE *ABDUCTED?*

I COULDN'T HEAR THE GENERAL THROUGH THE FORCE FIELD, COMMANDER GOR.

I COULDN'T EITHER, LIEUTENANT. BUT I COULD *SEE* HIM.

ZOD SAID TO ALL OF US, "I'LL *HELP* YOU. I *PROMISE.*"

ZOD AND LIEUTENANT URSA WERE BANISHED TO THE TREACHEROUS PHANTOM ZONE AS IF THEY WERE *COMMON CRIMINALS.*

THEY *ESCAPED* AND ATTEMPTED TO TAKE *CONTROL* OF THIS PRIMITIVE WORLD AND BUILD IT INTO NEW KRYPTON.

I AM CERTAIN I AM NOT THE ONLY KRYPTONIAN WONDERING--

--WHY DID KAL-EL *STOP* THEM?

EEEEERR

I MEAN THAT IN THE *LITERAL SENSE.*

THEY HELD A *VIGIL* IN YOUR HONOR AFTER YOU *"SACRIFICED"* YOURSELF DEFENDING EARTH FROM AN ALIEN INVASION.

CLANG CLANG

YET HERE YOU *ARE.* ALIVE AND WELL.

I'M NOT *WELL,* LUTHOR. NOTHING IS *WELL.*

HONG KONG.

FORTY-EIGHT HOURS AGO, OVER ONE HUNDRED THOUSAND KRYPTONIANS APPEARED ON EARTH.

SAN DIEGO.

HOW FAMILIAR ARE YOU WITH KANDOR, LUTHOR?

IF IT'S CONNECTED TO SUPERMAN, I *KNOW* ABOUT IT. KANDOR WAS A KRYPTONIAN METROPOLIS OF UNPARALLELED *CULTURE* AND *KNOWLEDGE.*

IT INSPIRED *OTHER* ALIEN SOCIETIES TO TAKE ITS NAME.

SUPERMAN AND SUPERGIRL DEALT WITH THOSE ON SEVERAL OCCASIONS.

BUT THE TRUE KRYPTONIAN CITY OF KANDOR WAS ABDUCTED, NEVER TO BE HEARD FROM AGAIN.

GENERAL SAMUEL LANE. CLEARANCE GRANTED.

VONK

UNTIL SUPERMAN HUNTED THIS CREATURE DOWN AND RETRIEVED KANDOR.

BRAINIAC?

HE'S LOOKING RATHER *FIT* THESE DAYS.

APPARENTLY HIS SHIP WAS KEEPING HIM THAT WAY. WITHOUT IT...HE'S STARTING TO SHOW SIGNS OF ATROPHY.

938013

SEVENTEEN MEN AND WOMEN HAVE *DIED* TRYING TO UNLOCK THE *DATA* TRAPPED IN THIS ALIEN'S *BRAIN*, LUTHOR.

I'D RATHER NOT LOSE ANY MORE OF MY OWN STAFF.

UNCHAIN ME AND I'LL GET TO WORK.

THE CHAINS STAY *ON*. YOU'RE A *CRIMINAL*.

AND THIS OPERATION OF YOURS IS AS *CLEAN* AS SUPERMAN'S VOCABULARY?

I'M HERE TO PROTECT THE WORLD.

SO AM *I*.

157

YOU AND I, GENERAL, WE'RE ALIKE I THINK, IN A *FEW* WAYS. TRUTH BE TOLD, YOU WERE ONE OF THE FIRST TO SEE WHAT *I* SEE IN SUPERMAN.

YOU AND I HAVE OUR *OWN* X-RAY VISION.

WHEN SUPERMAN INVADED METROPOLIS WITH THAT PERFECT *SMILE* AND FLUTTERING *CAPE*, YOU QUESTIONED HIS MOTIVES AS MUCH AS *I* DID.

AND YOU USED THE ENTIRE *U.S. MILITARY* TO DO IT.

EVEN THOUGH IT COST YOU THE VERY *PERSON* YOU WERE REALLY TRYING TO *PROTECT*.

YOUR *DAUGHTER*.

LOIS LANE.

LIKE ME, YOU'RE WILLING TO SACRIFICE WHATEVER IT *TAKES* TO RESCUE HUMANITY FROM THE *INFLUENCE* OF SUPERMAN.

BECAUSE AN ALIEN BEING WHO CAN CHANGE THE COURSE OF *RIVERS* MAKES HUMANITY *INSIGNIFICANT*.

HE HAS US REST ON OUR LAURELS AND CRY FOR *HELP* WHEN OUR CATS CLIMB TREES.

AND HE *CAPTURES* OUR DAUGHTERS' EYES WHILE MORE SUITABLE SUITORS ARE *IGNORED*.

IT'S A SHAME.

LOIS WASTED HER *BEST YEARS* ON SUPERMAN.

AND THEN, WHEN THE TIME FINALLY CAME, SHE HAD TO SCRAPE THE BOTTOM OF THE BARREL. SHE HAD TO *SETTLE* FOR A NAIVE SPELLCHECKER LIKE *CLARK KENT*.

THE VERY THOUGHT OF *MY* DAUGHTER *CHAINED* TO SOMEONE AS INEPT AS KENT IS MORE THAN I BELIEVE I COULD TAKE.

I MIGHT'VE EVEN *SNAPPED*.

BLAMM

YOU'LL EAT AT YOUR STATION.

YOU'LL KEEP THESE CHAINS ON.

AND YOU'LL NEVER, *EVER* MENTION MY DAUGHTER *AGAIN.*

DO YOU UNDERSTAND, LUTHOR?

I UNDERSTAND MORE THAN YOU, GENERAL LANE.

I'VE *SEEN* THE DAMAGE *ONE* BEING LIKE SUPERMAN HAS DONE TO OUR WORLD. YOU MULTIPLY THAT BY *ONE HUNDRED THOUSAND* AND WE'LL ALL BE *SLAVES,* WORSHIPPING THE AIR THEY FLY IN.

I'LL BREAK OPEN BRAINIAC'S MIND, BUT I'LL NEED MORE *WEAPONS* TO END THIS INVASION.

YOU THINK I'M PUTTING *ALL* OF MY CHIPS ON AN EGOTISTICAL SADIST LIKE *YOU?*

YOU'RE ONLY *ONE* BULLET IN MY GUN, LUTHOR.

I HAVE A LOT OF OTHERS.

"AND THEY'RE MUCH *BIGGER* THAN YOU."

METROPOLIS.

ALURA?

YOU'RE THE LEADER OF KANDOR'S SECURITY, THARA. *FINISH* THE EVACUATION--

--WHILE MY HUSBAND AND I HELP OUR DAUGHTER AND OUR NEPHEW.

REMEMBER TO BE *DELICATE.* THESE CREATURES ARE *FRAGILE.*

THIS WAY, MR. PRESIDENT--

BY GOD, AGENT LIBERTY. THAT'S THE MONSTER THAT *KILLED* SUPERMAN.

UNITED STATES

I'D SAY THINGS ARE A LITTLE MORE IN SUPERMAN'S FAVOR *TODAY.*

CITY PARK

"DOOMSDAY IS DEAD."

"YES. ZOR-EL AND ALURA THINK THEY CAN LEAD KANDOR TO SAFETY."

BUT THEY ARE ONLY *SCIENTISTS*. AND WHAT *HAPPENED* TO KRYPTON THE *LAST* TIME IT WAS LED BY SCIENTISTS?

IT *EXPLODED*, COMMANDER.

I CAN'T HELP BUT *QUESTION* KAL-EL'S DEDICATION TO KRYPTON. HE SPENDS FAR TOO MUCH TIME FILLING THIS TRADITIONAL SANCTUARY OF REFLECTION ON THE EVE OF *WAR*--

--WITH STRANGE *TRINKETS* FROM HIS TERRESTRIAL EXPERIENCES.

MOST OF KANDOR MIGHT NOT SEE WHAT WE DO, LIEUTENANT, BUT AFTER THE UNLEASHING OF *DOOMSDAY* TODAY--

--THERE IS NO DOUBT IN MY *MIND*.

NOTHING A LITTLE NATURAL *TACTILE-TELEKINESIS* CAN'T HANDLE.

KRAKK

FWAKK

IF *ANY* OF GENERAL ZOD'S SOLDIERS TRY TO *FREE* THAT LUNATIC--

FUMP